13

Sea horses suck in their food through their mouths. Their mouths are shaped like tubes. Sea horses eat baby fish and tiny plants and animals called **plankton** (PLANK-tuhn).

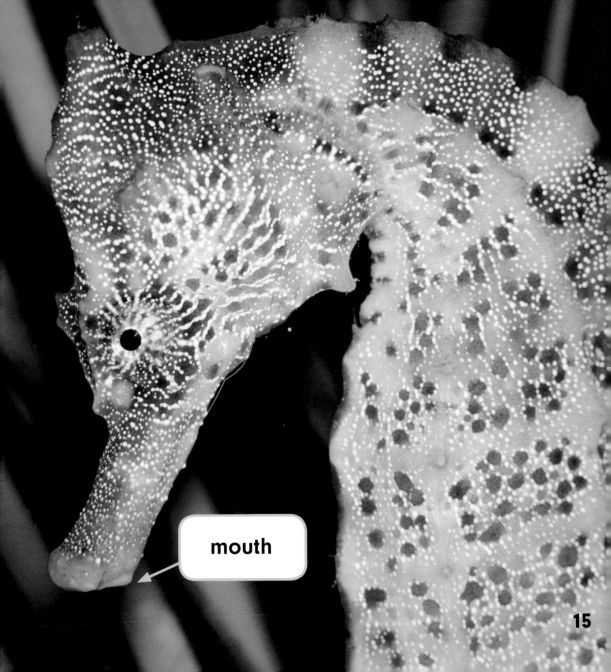

mouth

Sea horses come in colors from pale yellow to bright red. They can change color to match their background. That helps them hide from enemies.

A Daddy and His Babies

Most female animals have babies. Among sea horses, however, the males give birth! First, a male and a female dance side by side. Then the female sea horse puts her eggs in the male's **pouch**.

pouch

The eggs grow into tiny sea horses inside the pouch. After a few weeks, the baby sea horses come out and float away in the sea. Sea horse superdads have hundreds of babies at once!

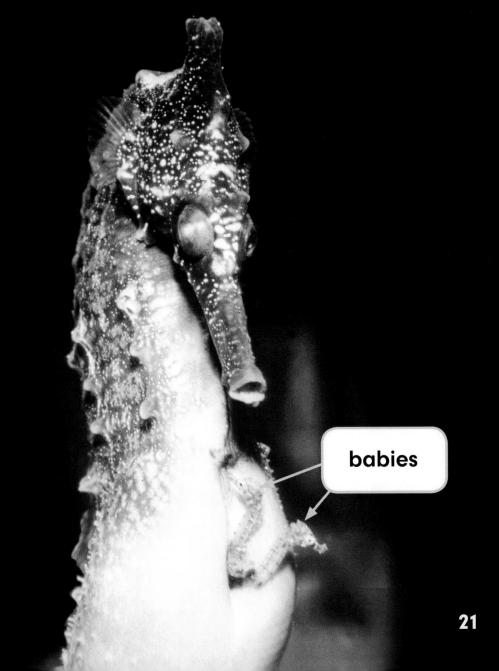

babies

Glossary

crown: a round piece of skin on the top of a sea horse's head

fins: wing-like body parts of fish, used for swimming and steering in water

plankton: tiny animals and plants that float in water

pouch: a pocket-like body part

For More Information

Books

Seahorse Reef: A Story of the South Pacific.
Smithsonian Oceanic Collection. Sally M. Walker
(Smithsonian Books, 2007)

Seahorses. Animals Animals (series). Steven Otfinoski
(Marshall Cavendish, 2007)

Web Sites

Monterey Bay Aquarium: Saving Seahorses in the Sea
www.montereybayaquarium.org/efc/efc_se/se_ssh_sea.asp
Learn fun facts about sea horses. Click on the links
for pictures.

Nova Online: Kingdom of the Seahorse
www.pbs.org/wgbh/nova/seahorse
Learn about different sea horses, their bodies, and
their babies.

Index

birth 18, 20
color 16
crown 6
eggs 18, 20
enemies 16
fins 10
food 12, 14

head 4, 6
mouth 14
plankton 14
plates 8
pouch 18, 20
skin 8
swimming 4, 10

About the Author

A writer and editor for 25 years, Valerie Weber especially loves working in children's publishing. The variety of topics is endless, from weird animals to making movies. It is her privilege to try to engage children in their world through books.